21st Century Junior Library

INFOGRAPHICS: ON THE SCOREBOARD

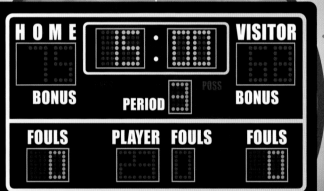

HOME   VISITOR

BONUS   PERIOD   BONUS

FOULS   PLAYER   FOULS   FOULS

HOME RUN!!!
BATTER   BALL   STRIKE   OUT

Sports-Graphics Jr.

Heather Williams

Published in the United States of America by:

CHERRY LAKE PRESS
2395 South Huron Parkway, Suite 200, Ann Arbor, Michigan 48104
www.cherrylakepress.com

Reading Adviser: Beth Walker Gambro, MS, Ed., Reading Consultant, Yorkville, IL

Photo Credits: © hvostik/Shutterstock, © artisticco/Getty Images, © msan10/Getty Images, © FARBAI/Getty Images, cover; © Jessica Orozco, 5; © Jessica Orozco, 7; © Jessica Orozco, 8; © Jessica Orozco, 9; © Jessica Orozco, 10; © Jessica Orozco, 11; © Jessica Orozco, 13; © Jessica Orozco, 14; © Jessica Orozco, 16; © Jessica Orozco, 17; © Jessica Orozco, 20; © Jessica Orozco, 21

Cherry Lake Press is an imprint of Cherry Lake Publishing Group.

Library of Congress Cataloging-in-Publication Data has been filed and is available at catalog.loc.gov.

Cherry Lake Publishing Group would like to acknowledge the work of the Partnership for 21st Century Learning, a Network of Battelle for Kids. Please visit Battelle for Kids online for more information.

Printed in the United States of America

Note from publisher: Websites change regularly, and their future contents are outside of our control. Supervise children when conducting any recommended online searches for extended learning opportunities.

ABOUT THE AUTHOR

Heather Williams is a former English teacher and school librarian. She has a passion for seeing readers of all ages connect with others through stories and experiences. Heather has written more than 50 books for children. She enjoys walking her dog, reading, and watching sports. She lives in North Carolina with her husband and two children.

CHERRY LAKE PRESS

CONTENTS

What's the Score?   4

Getting on the Board   6

How to Score More   12

Changing the Scoring Game   15

Who's on Top?   18

   Activity   22

   Find Out More   23

   Glossary   24

   Index   24

WHAT'S THE SCORE?

People around the world love sports. But a true sports fan knows a game is more fun when their team comes out on top.

Winning may not be everything. But a win is a lot of fun. And winning can't happen without scoring. Every sport has a set of rules for how to earn points. Whether a team scores one goal or 26 runs, there's only one winner when the game is over.

FOUR OF PRO SPORTS' HIGHEST-SCORING GAMES

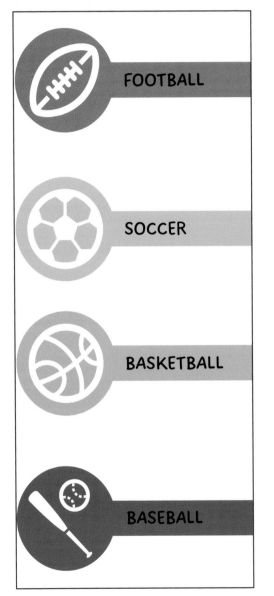

FOOTBALL

SOCCER

BASKETBALL

BASEBALL

WASHINGTON COMMANDERS VS. NEW YORK GIANTS

72–41, November 27, 1966 (National Football League)

AUSTRALIA VS. AMERICAN SAMOA

31–0, April 11, 2001 (International Soccer)

DETROIT PISTONS VS. DENVER NUGGETS

186–184, December 13, 1983 (National Basketball Association)

PHILADELPHIA PHILLIES VS. CHICAGO CUBS

26–23, August 25, 1922 (Major League Baseball)

GETTING ON THE BOARD

Some sports are played by a team. Soccer, baseball, and hockey are examples. Teams play against other teams. They compete in **leagues.** Countries have teams that play in **tournaments** like the World Cup and the Olympics.

Other sports are individual. One player might play against another. Tennis is like this. In other individual sports, athletes do tasks to earn points. They take part in **competitions.** Gymnastics and figure skating are examples. Whatever the sport, whoever has the best score wins!

GOAL SPORTS

In these sports, players score by getting an object over a line or into a special area, called a goal. A goal is worth one point in hockey and soccer. In basketball, a goal is worth two or three points. A touchdown in football is worth six points.

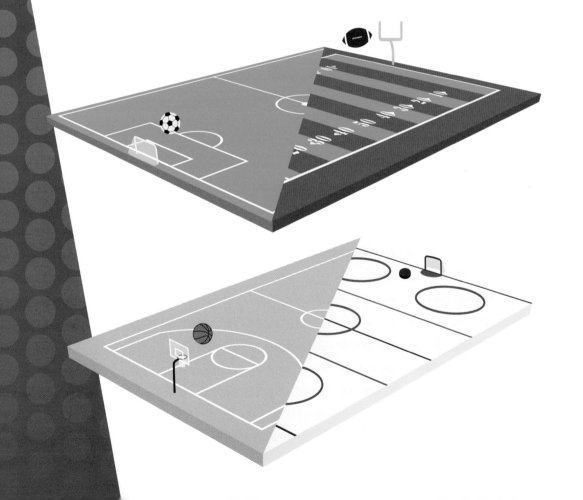

HOW TO SCORE A GAME OF TENNIS

NUMBER OF POINTS	CORRESPONDING CALL
0	Love
1	15
2	30
3	40
4	Game
Tied at 15	15 All
Tied at 30	30 All
Tied at 40	Deuce

SWING, HIT, RUN!: BASEBALL SCORING

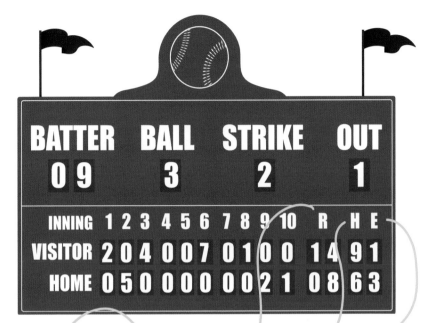

BATTER	BALL	STRIKE	OUT
0 9	3	2	1

INNING	1	2	3	4	5	6	7	8	9	10	R	H	E
VISITOR	2	0	4	0	0	7	0	1	0	0	14	9	1
HOME	0	5	0	0	0	0	0	2	1	0	8	6	3

R (RUN)
when a batter crosses home plate, a run is awarded; a run is one point, and the team with the most runs wins

E (ERROR)
a mistake by the **defensive** team that gives the batting team an advantage

H (HIT)
when a batter hits the ball and makes it to a base

SMALLEST NUMBER WINS!

Running is a sport where the biggest number is not the best score. It doesn't matter if a race is long or short. The runner who finishes in the shortest amount of time is the winner.

5K

The 5K is a common road race. It is around 3 miles (4.8 km) long. Most runners complete a 5K in 30 to 40 minutes.

MARATHON

A marathon is 26.2 miles (42.2 kilometers) long. In 2022, 22,580 people ran in the Boston Marathon. Most runners complete a marathon in 4 to 5 hours.

100-METER SPRINT

The 100-meter (328-foot) sprint is a common race. It is used in elementary school PE classes and in the Olympic Games.

HOW TO SCORE MORE

Every sport has a basic way to score. Most sports also have ways to score even more. Players in some individual sports can add extra moves or tricks. Most team sports have overtime or extra time. This allows more time to break a tie. Sometimes a soccer game is still tied after overtime. Then they have a **penalty shootout.** Baseball games have extra innings if there is a tie. In some sports, **fouls** also give teams a chance to score more.

EXTRA POINTS IN FOOTBALL

EXTRA POINT
The kicker earns one point by kicking the ball through the goalposts.

TWO-POINT CONVERSION
The quarterback or another player earns two points by scoring another touchdown from the two-yard line.

SAFETY
The other team earns two points when a player is tackled or drops the ball in their own end zone.

FREE KICK!

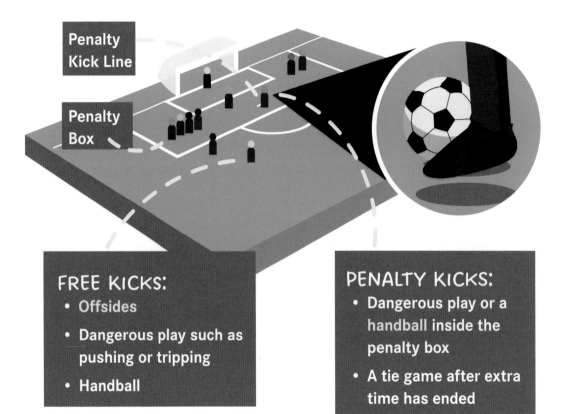

Penalty Kick Line

Penalty Box

FREE KICKS:
- Offsides
- Dangerous play such as pushing or tripping
- Handball

PENALTY KICKS:
- Dangerous play or a handball inside the penalty box
- A tie game after extra time has ended

CHANGING THE SCORING GAME

Technology has changed how people play sports. Many games are played in front of cameras. Some are even attached to drones. These "extra eyes" make it easy to stop and replay moments in games. A few big moments in sports history might have been different with modern tools.

INSTANT REPLAY

1. THE PLAY
Was the player out of bounds?

2. REVIEW
The main **referee** looks at slowed-down videos to check.

3. DISCUSSION
All of the referees meet to discuss the play. Then the main referee talks to the coaches.

4. DECISION
The main referee announces the final ruling.

VIDEO ASSISTANT REFEREE (VAR)

- There are four referees on the field during a FIFA soccer game.
  - For VAR, a team of three people are in a video room. They view film and review calls made by the main referee.

OFFSIDES

- FIFA first used VAR in 2018.
- In the 2022 World Cup, VAR reviewed every goal.
- New offsides technology was used in the 2022 World Cup. It can show if any part of a player is offsides, even a kneecap or the tip of a shoe.

WHO'S ON TOP?

Most, first, fastest, best! Every sport has a list of records. Many of those records are based on scoring. Some records are set by teams. Others are set by individual athletes. Some records are even considered unbreakable.

Setting a record is a big deal for an athlete. It usually means they are the best in their sport. Breaking a record is a big deal, too. Working hard to score goals, touchdowns, or three-pointers makes a great athlete even more memorable.

SERENA WILLAMS, GREATEST OF ALL TIME

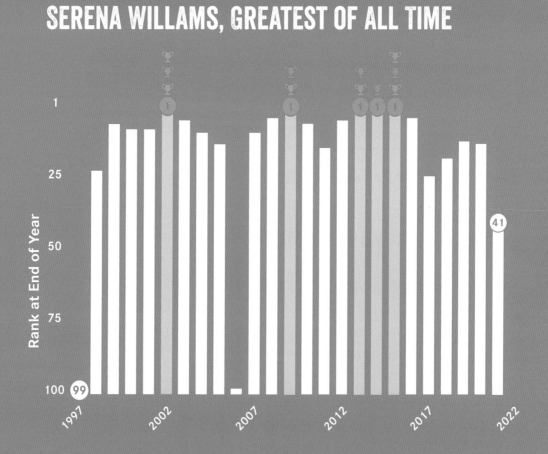

Serena Williams retired in 2022 after one of the most successful careers of any athlete in any sport.

- She won 23 major titles—the most ever by a woman.
- In 14 of the 26 years she played, her win percentage was 80 or higher.
- She beat 306 different players from 50 countries.
- She competed in four Olympics and won four gold medals.

19

WHERE RECORDS ARE MADE

KAREEM ABDUL-JABBAR, BASKETBALL

38,387 career points in the NBA

RICKEY HENDERSON, BASEBALL

2,295 career runs in MLB

CA

TIGER WOODS, GOLF

20 career holes-in-one

DIANA TAURASI, BASKETBALL

9,693 career points in the WNBA

2022, Tiger Woods; 2021, NBA Media Ventures; 2021, Fadeaway World

STEPHEN CURRY, BASKETBALL
3,220 career three-pointers made in the NBA

ABBY WAMBACH, SOCCER
184 career goals for the U.S. Women's National Team

WI

IL

KY

OH

NY

PA

NJ

MS

MARY SLANEY, TRACK
fastest mile by an American woman (4 minutes, 16.71 seconds)

WILT CHAMBERLAIN, BASKETBALL
only NBA player in history to score 100 points in a single game

JERRY RICE, FOOTBALL
208 career touchdowns in the NFL

TYSON GAY, TRACK
fastest men's 100-meter run (9.69 seconds)

ACTIVITY

How Many Ways to Score?

One of the highest-scoring NFL games of all time took place on November 27, 1966. The Washington Commanders beat the New York Giants 72–41. How many different ways could these teams have gotten to the final score?

Materials Needed

- Writing utensil
- Paper
- Calculator (if needed)

Scoring Guide

- Safety = 2 points
- 1 Field Goal = 3 points
- 1 Touchdown = 6 points
- Extra Point(s) / Try After Touchdown
  > Field Goal = 1 point
  > 2-point Conversion = 2 points

1. Start with the Giants. Divide the final score by 6 to see how many touchdowns may have been possible. 41/6 = 6 with 5 left over

2. Look at the left over points. They may have come from 5 extra point field goals. They might also have come from 1 field goal and 1 safety.

3. Use this example to figure out at least three different ways the Commanders scored their game-winning 72 points.

FIND OUT MORE

Books

Caissie, David. *Sports.* Hollywood, FL: Mason Crest, 2022.

Hawkes, Chris. *My Encyclopedia of Very Important Sports.* New York: DK Publishing, 2020.

Ricci, Nick. *Score Points!* New York: Scholastic, 2016.

Online Resources to Explore with an Adult

Britannica Kids: Sports

Kiddle: Sport Facts for Kids

Bibliography

Rookie Road. "How Does Scoring Work in Sports?" 2022.

Sports Reference. 2022.

GLOSSARY

competitions (com-puh-TIH-shunz) events where people play against each other in an effort to win

defensive (dih-FEN-siv) working to prevent the other team from scoring

fouls (FOWLZ) actions that are against the rules

handball (HAND-bawl) when a soccer player's hands or arms touch the ball

leagues (LEEGZ) organized groups of sports teams that play against each other

offsides (OFF-sydz) when a player receiving a pass in soccer is closer to the goal than the last defender on the other team

penalty shootout (PEN-uhl-tee SHOOT-owt) a tiebreaker in soccer in which each team gets five penalty shots; the team with the most shots wins the game

referee (ref-uh-REE) a person who watches players to make sure they are following the rules

tournaments (TUR-nuh-muntz) series of sports games that are played close together to find overall winners

win percentage (WIN pur-SEN-tij) the percent of games that a player or team has won; win percentage is calculated as number of wins / total number of games played

INDEX

baseball, 5–6, 9, 12, 20

Curry, Stephen, 21

hockey, 6–7

National Basketball League (NBA), 5, 20–2

Olympics, 6, 11, 19
overtime, 12

soccer, 5–7, 12, 17, 21

Women's National Basketball Association (WNBA) 20
World Cup, 6, 17